PAINTING FOR PEACE IN FERGUSON

CAROL SWARTOUT KLEIN

"When I was a boy and I would see scary things on the news, my mother would say to me 'Look for the helpers. You will always find people who are helping.'"

Fred Rogers
The World According to Mister Rogers

Published by Layla Dog Press, an imprint of Blank Slate Communications LLC, St. Louis, MO 63110
For more information, visit www.paintingforpeacebook.com

Design Team: Robert O'Neil and Michael Kilfoy
Cover Calligraphy: Marie Enger
Photography: Michael Kilfoy, Ryan Archer, Rubin Roche, Carol Swartout Klein, Jody Porter, Gussie Klorer, Dan Duncan, Kelley Ray and Robin Shively

Printed in the United States. Library of Congress Control Number: 2015930142
ISBN: 978-0-9898671-5-3 Paperback
ISBN: 978-0-9898671-6-0 Hardback

Dedicated to the people of Ferguson and St. Louis as they begin the steps of healing and creating a stronger and better community

In the small town of Ferguson
In 2014
Some people did things that
Were meaner than mean

Some people were mad
Some people were sad
But everyone, everywhere
Felt pretty bad 😞

Police were there
And protesters too
People were scared
Didn't know what to do

Some locked their doors
Boarded windows up tight
To help keep them safe
All through the long night

But when morning came
Folks took one look around
And said we don't like
The looks of our town

We have an idea
We know what to do
We'll bring out our paints
Red, Yellow and Blue

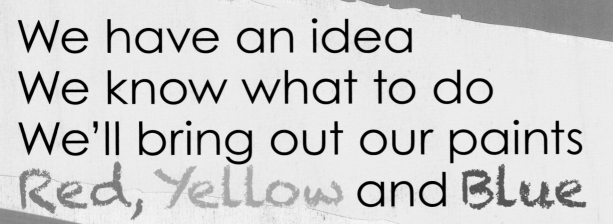

We'll *Paint* up those boards

That make us feel down

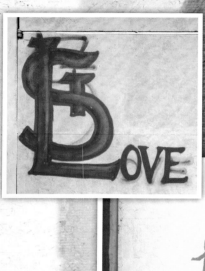

We'll paint pictures of **LOVE**

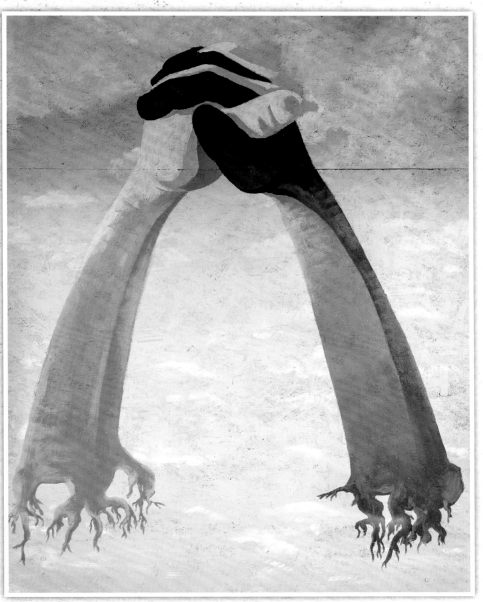

And bring **HOPE** to the town

And so they came out
On a day Sunny and Bright

Young folks And old folks

Black folks And white

They went up to the North

WE ALL ♥ FERGUSON

And down **South** near Shaw

With their *Paints* and their brushes

And started to Draw

They drew pictures of Peace

Of **Hope** and of **Light**

23

That show Love's even stronger

Than the **Darkest** of nights

Some art had sayings

JUSTICE IS WHAT LOVE LOOKS LIKE IN PUBLIC

THEY THOUGHT THEY COULD BURY US...

THEY DIDN'T KNOW

WE WERE SEEDS

CENTER of Hope AND Peace

STILL WE RISE

With **Words** that have power

Other art was from Nature

Long Live the Rose that that grew from the Concrete When no one else even cared.....

A Tree, Bird or Flower

Some Dazzled with Colors

That Danced in the light

Other art was more Bold

By Kaite D.

"think of all the BEAUTY Still Left around you and be happy"

PRAY FOR OUR CITY!/WORLD!

ONE LOVE!

...it's the answer!

Shine YOUR Light

#callmerrartworks

309

32

Using just **Black** and **White**

As they walked down the street

They were *Proud* of their art

'Cause for things to get better

We must Each do our part

SOUTH **STL**
LOVES
FERGUSON

THE OPPOSITE OF WAR ISNT PEACE IT'S CREATION

As we work side by side

And 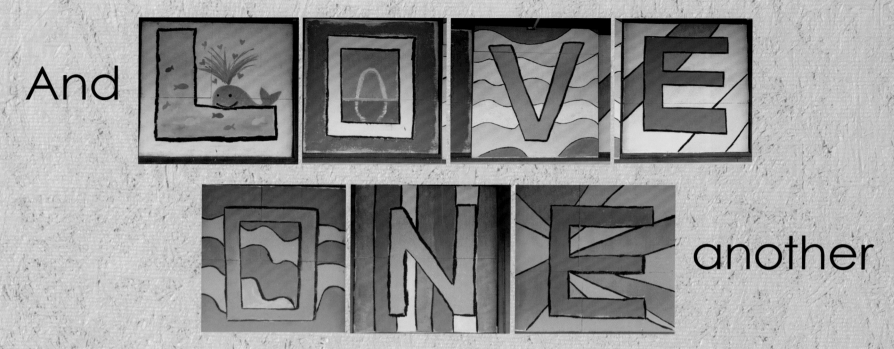 another

Both **IN** and **OUT**-side

The Work is not finished

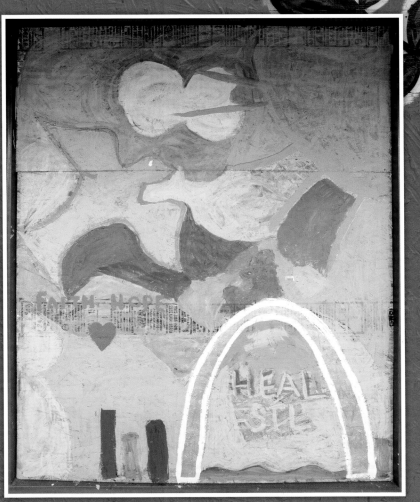

There's much more to be done

PEACE   LOVE   IMO'S

PEACE LOVE

STRENGTH

OPEN

AMANI-RENAS

TAYTU BETUL

I HAVE DECIDED
TO Stick WITH LOVE
HATE IS TOO GREAT
A BURDEN TO BEAR.
~MLK JR

I ♥ Ferg

Be the CHANGE

SHALOM

INJUSTICE ANYWHERE IS A
THREAT TO JUSTICE
everywhere

Believe There Is Good In The World

ONE ♥ LOVE

"A JOURNEY OF A
THOUSAND MILES
BEGINS WITH A
SINGLE STEP."
-LAO TZU

"Great Leaders define Reality and give HOPE."
Peace Love

United We Stand. DIVIDED WE FALL

PEACE & LOVE

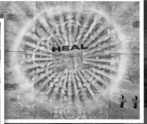

HEAL

PEACE

UNITY

LETS HEAL

But this **Art** shows the **Spirit...**

PEACE
WE WILL RISE
IT'S IN OUR HANDS
♥Ferguson

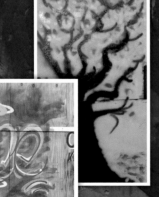

Peace

FERGUSON STRONG

All we Need is Love

Of a new Ferguson

BEFORE

AFTER

Painting for Peace

was inspired by artists and business owners who wanted to do something positive for their city after months of anger and uncertainty. The artists started by painting boarded up windows in South St. Louis and then continued in Ferguson following the unrest in November 2014. Within days after the destruction and continuing for several weeks despite cold weather, volunteers, artists, church youth groups and whole families painted block after block of boarded up businesses with artwork that ranged from childlike to thought provoking and compelling works of art. As businesses have repaired their damage, most of the boards have come down.

This book will continue to capture this brief spontaneous moment of hope and goodwill as a community came together to move in a new direction.

Painting for Peace

would like to thank all those who made such a difference in our community. Although we have attempted to capture as many names as possible of those who participated we recognize that many may have been missed.

We will be updating the list online so please contact us at: paintingforpeace.book@gmail.com if you were involved and want to be included online or in future editions.

Thanks to the Artists and Volunteers who were a part of Painting For Peace

Rachel Abbinanti
Rosie Abramczyk
Phil & Gail Aho
Joey Albanese
Dawn Anglin
Leah, Lou, Eliot, Dennis & Philip Bailey
Tina Bailey & family
Ellie Balk
Carla Bond Baranowski
Elizabeth & Theresa Baranowski
Keith Bazier
Jonel Beach
Noelle Becker
Dominique Begnaud
Phil, Lydia, Stacia & Theresa Berwick
Ana & Gabe Bonfili
James Bonsanti
Nathan Bookout
Mike Brandon
Alex Braun
Dr. Crystal & April Breeden Peairs
Anthony Brescia
Kim Bromeier
Deneishea Bryant
Janice & Jade Bugett-Hygrade
Joan & Julie Bugnitz
Karen Bult
Mary Beth Bussen
Christina Carroll
Breanna Cashel
Angela Catchings
Lisa & Sophia Chabot
Diedre & Felice Chatman
Sherri Chisholm
Marnie Claunch
Adam Cook
Andy, Linda, Sarah & Emily Cross
Thomas Culler
Fabia D'Amore-Krug
Carly Davis
Damon Davis

Kareem Deanes
Isabella & Sophia DeFord
Veronica Delgado
Allison Dent
Blaine Deutsch & Laura Neuwirth
Kalyn & Julia Neuwirth-Deutsch
Aaron Dickerson
Dahven White & Allen Doctor
Reid, Chase & Moxie Doctor
Sarah, Jack, Taylor & Katie Donato
Kiley Donovan
Dan Duncan
Monica Brendel Duwel
Darcy, Eddie & Val Edwin
Rebecca Eilering
Meredith Elkin
Krista Estes
Laila & Parisa Faramarzi
Renee Farmar
Rebecca Fehlig & Family
Eleonore Fischer
Liza Fishbone
LeAnn Fisher
Brian Flynn
Rebecca & Meg Flynn
Lancelot Fordyce III
Elyse & Tyler Frazier
Sarah Carmen Geiss
Karen Gold
Sheri Goldsmith
Shine Goodie
Abby Gordon
Dana Gray
Kurt Greenbaum
Kevin Gregory
Allison Hake
Mikey, Genevieve & Cecilia Halaska
Cheyenne & Quron Harris

Onnie Harrison
Dianne Hartle
Adrienne Hawkins
Mary Belth Heiligenstein
Amanda Helman
Dixie Herrington
Alison Armstrong Hillman
Theresa Hopkins
Tara Howarth
Tracy Hudson
Albert & ZoeyAnn Huff
Jason Hunt
Rita Hunt
Zaire Imani
Meagan Impellizzeri
Emily Davis & Dwayne Isgrig
Isiah, Zeke & Naomi Davis-Isgrig
Carly Jacobs
Loren Jenks
Diana Johnson
Angela Jones
Elizabeth Knight
Rob Knight
Laura Knoblock
Darci & Stasie Knowles
Mary Krummenacher
Josh, Eavan & Ansel Kryah
Jen Kubiszewski
SirGabriel Laplander
Stephanie Larimer
Tom & Kim Litton
Susan Logsdon
Lucia & Sofia Lonero
Charlene Lopez
Jennifer, Mikie, Joey & Gabe Lumetta
Heidi Lung
Tammy Turner Maclean
Annie Martineau
Jordan Massey
Ja'Mel McCaine
Andrea McMurray
Kimberly Lorrene Melahn

Carrie Meyer
Kristen Middeke
Magdaline Middeke
Jeff Miller
Joe Mohr
Anne Moore
Katelyn Moore
April, Brenda & May Morrison
Shuka Moshiri
Racquel Mosley
Dawn, Grace, Nate & Stephen Murphy
Robin, Mac, Seda & Daegan Murphy
Merle, Cynthia & Parris Nathan
Marcela Navarrete
Joyce Neikirk
Eric Wolfgang & Brittany Nelson
Emma Nowlin
Darius Overbey
Christine Palmer
Brandon Pappert
Megan Glori Parker
Anastasia Parks
Donald, Amanda, Don Jr. & Demetrius Partee
Libby Pedersen
Laura Pennington
Nelson Perez, Jr.
Ryan Pier
Shannon Piva Piwowarczyk
Frank Popper
Jody Porter
Cheryl Punzalan
Michael & Julie Quintero
Kelley Ray
Isabelle Raymond
Richard & Karen Norman Reilly
Sarah Anne Rennie
Molly Rodgers
Grace Rogers
AJ Rosenberg

Lauren Rundquist
Becky Kern-Ryan
Avi, Ethan & Lissie Ryan
Chris Sabatino
Paul Sager
Lisa Sanditz
Jenn Sarti
Laurel Schmitt
Kristin Serafini
Theodosia & Paisley Sessen
Mary Shay
Alex Sheen
Elizabeth Simons
Jason Skrbec
Natalie & Alex Smithey
Maurice St. Pierre
Emily Stafford
Keith Stephens
Jennifer Stiller
Tessa Stoverink
Jon Strauser
Mark Swain
George Taylor
Amina Terry
The Thayer Family
Lavette Thomas
Reggie Thomas
Mary Timmel
Anya Toler
Logan Trupiano
Hyanneke van der Pennen
Jenny Walker
Elysia Webber
Moe Weiss
Anna, Maddie & Culeen Wenger
Maggie Wheelock
Meghan Kearney White
Autumn Wiggins
Dale Wilke
David & Peggy Williamson
Amber Withycombe
Peat Wollaeger
Jonny Xacto

Ferguson Strong

A Special Thanks to the following who made the citywide Paint for Peace effort a reality

Gail Babcock	Dana Sebastian-Duncan	Mike and Lizzie Lonero	Cafe Natasha
Chris Bellers	Catherine Gilbert	Bob McGartland	Dick Blick Art Materials
Natasha Bahrami	Alderwoman Megan Green	Jeff and Carey Morgan	Ferguson Youth Initiative
Martin Casas	Tom Halaska, Jr.	Maria Price	The Ferguson Response
Jenny Churchill	Alderwoman Christine Ingrassia	Christopher Shearman	Grand Center Arts Academy
Alderman Steve Conway	Dwayne James	Rachel Witt	Paint for Peace
Laura Coppinger	Gussie Klorer	ArtBar	Vincenzo's Restaurant
	Jen Kubiszewski	Artmart	

About the Author

Carol Swartout Klein – grew up in Ferguson, and was so inspired by witnessing the spirit of hundreds of volunteers coming together to bring hope to a community in shock that she wanted to capture the story and *Painting for Peace in Ferguson* is the result. A journalist and marketing professional by training Klein always wanted to do a children's book. She saw how the actual process of creating the artwork was healing for all those involved … as the community came together to help others, the artists, business owners and volunteers actually benefitted themselves … and created new connections that she hopes will continue in the future.

Proceeds from the book will benefit art and youth programs and small business recovery in north St. Louis County. Additional tax deductible donations may be made to the Painting for Peace project through the Greater St. Louis Community Foundation. For more information please visit www.paintingforpeacebook.com